DISCARDED

Humorous Hi Jinx

PRANKS to Play at School

Megan Cooley Peterson

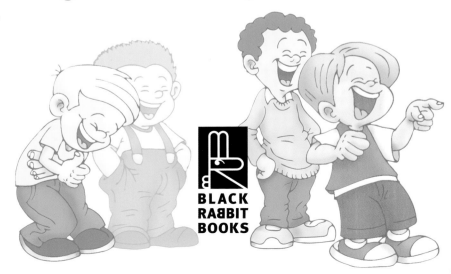

BLACK RABBIT BOOKS

Hi Jinx is published by Black Rabbit Books
P.O. Box 3263, Mankato, Minnesota, 56002.
www.blackrabbitbooks.com
Copyright © 2018 Black Rabbit Books

Marysa Storm, editor; Michael Sellner, designer;
Catherine Cates, production designer;
Omay Ayres, photo researcher

Library of Congress Cataloging-in-Publication Data
Names: Peterson, Megan Cooley, author.
Title: Pranks to play at school /
by Megan Cooley Peterson.
Description: Mankato, Minnesota : Black Rabbit Books,
[2018] | Series: Hi jinx. Humorous hi jinx | Includes
bibliographical references and index.
Identifiers: LCCN 2017007256 (print) |
LCCN 2017024150 (ebook) | ISBN 9781680723649
(e-book) | ISBN 9781680723342 (library binding)
Subjects: LCSH: Practical jokes–Juvenile literature. |
Tricks–Juvenile literature.
Classification: LCC PN6231.P67 (ebook) |
LCC PN6231.P67 P48 2018 (print) | DDC 818/.602-dc23
LC record available at https://lccn.loc.gov/2017007256

Printed in China. 9/17

Image Credits

Contents

Chapter 1

School Days

Want to move to the head of the class? Pull these pranks! Hallways and classrooms are perfect pranking spots. Just don't forget to study between jokes.

The Prankster's Guide

Playing pranks should not get you grounded for life! Follow this guide to keep your pranks safe and fun.

1. The Target
Choose someone who enjoys pranks.

2. Nice Is Best
The best pranks aren't embarrassing.

3. Keep It Clean
Making fake vomit is fun. Leaving a mess for someone else to clean up is not!

4. Safety First
Could your prank hurt a person, animal, or property? If so, choose a new prank.

An **Austrian** palace has trick fountains.
They spray people walking by.

6

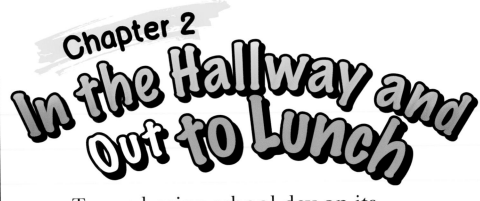

Chapter 2
In the Hallway and Out to Lunch

Turn a boring school day on its head. First, grab a dollar bill. Tape fishing line to one end. Then put the money in the hallway. When someone tries to grab it, yank it away!

Pull My Finger

Start the day with a prank. At home, make your knuckle look hurt. At school, hold your finger in your jacket. Tell your friends you slammed it in your locker door. Give them quick peeks of your **busted** knuckle.

How to Make a Broken Knuckle

Step 1
Grab some modeling wax. Be sure to read the package's directions. Stick a ball of wax on your knuckle. Smooth it out. It should look like part of your finger.

Step 2
Cover the wax with skin-tone paint.

Step 3
Carefully cut into the wax with a plastic knife. The cut should run across the knuckle.

Step 4
Drop fake blood into the cut. Let the blood dry.

Old black-and-white movies used chocolate syrup as fake blood.

What's My Number?

Switch your friends' locker numbers.
First, take a photo of the numbers.
Cut the photos to the same size as the
locker numbers. Tape the photos out
of order over the real numbers. Wait
until your friends are at their lockers.
Then say, "I don't think that's
your locker!" Will they
believe you?

Unwanted Guest

Hide a fake snake inside a friend's locker. Tuck it into a book or folder. Watch your friend pull it out. Stand back in case your target freaks out.

Broken Straws

Trick your friends at lunch. Poke small holes at the tops of some straws. Then give them to your friends. They'll try to drink. And the straws won't work.

Get a Grip

Don't throw away your used napkin. Use it in a prank! Secretly wet your napkin with water. Hide it in your palm. Then ask if anyone wants to arm wrestle. You'll win when your target feels the goo.

A teacher once pranked a student who fell asleep during class. The teacher had the entire class leave the room! When the student woke up, he was all alone.

14

Chapter 3
Head of the Class

Time to toss out the seating chart! Before class starts, have your classmates switch desks. Have everyone sit one desk away from their usual spot. See how long it takes your teacher to notice.

Low Five?

A desk holds paper, books, and pencils. But what about fake arms? Slip a fake arm into your desk. It should stick out. Tuck one of your arms into your shirt. Then lean over the desk. Tell your target you smashed your arm.

Extra Credit

Have a friend who went on vacation? Welcome him or her back with a fake worksheet. Drop the homework off at his or her house. Try not to laugh when your friend hands it in.

17

Chapter 4

In the Bathroom

Toilet Trouble

Head into the bathroom. Place "Out of Order" signs on all the stalls. Watch as people read the signs and look confused. Tell them they'll have to pee their pants. Just don't pee yours laughing!

Chapter 5
Get in on the Hi Jinx

Many **senior** classes pull pranks. Seniors at a high school in California took their prank to another level. They hired a **mariachi** band! The band played music while following the principal around.

You don't have to wait until you're older to pull school pranks! Push up your sleeves. You're ready to prank it up at school now.

Take It One Step More

1. Are there ever times when playing pranks isn't **appropriate**? Why or why not?

2. **What kind of fake homework could you make for a friend?**

3. Choose your favorite prank from the book. How can you improve it?

GLOSSARY

appropriate (uh-PROH-pree-it)—right or suited for some purpose or situation

Austrian (AW-stree-uhn)—someone or something from the country Austria

bust (BUHST)—to break or smash, especially with force

mariachi (mahr-ee-AH-chee)—a type of lively Mexican street music played by a band of trumpets and guitars

senior (SEEN-yer)—relating to students in their final year of high school or college

tone (TOHN)—a tint or shade of color

BOOKS

Owen, Ruth. *Pranks, Tricks, and Practical Jokes.* DIY for Boys. New York: PowerKids Press, 2014.

Peterson, Megan Cooley. *Pranks to Play around Town.* Humorous Hi Jinx. Mankato, MN: Black Rabbit Books, 2018.

Winterbottom, Julie. *Pranklopedia: The Funniest, Grossest, Craziest, Not-Mean Pranks on the Planet!* New York: Workman Publishing, 2013.

WEBSITES

Jokes and Riddles
www.funology.com/jokes-and-riddles/

Perfect Pranks
www.fun-stuff-to-do.com/perfectpranks.html

INDEX